I0444759

I'M NOT SHY

HOW TO OVERCOME SHYNESS, SOCIAL
ANXIETY, AND BEING AN INTROVERT

JONATHAN GREEN

Edited by
ALICE FOGLIATA

DRAGON GOD BOOKS

Copyright © 2018 by Dragon God, Inc.

All rights reserved.

Simultaneously published in United States of America, the UK, India, Germany, France, Italy, Canada, Japan, Spain, and Brazil.

All rights reserved. No part of this book may be reproduced in any form or by any other electronic or mechanical means – except in the case of brief quotations embedded in articles or reviews –without written permission from its author.

I'm Not Shy has provided the most accurate information possible. Many of the techniques used in this book are from personal experiences. The author shall not be held liable for any damages resulting from use of this book.

Paperback ISBN: 9781718077676

CONTENTS

Don't Go it Alone	v
Introduction	vii

PART I
EXPLORING SHYNESS AND SOCIAL ANXIETY

1. Are You an Introvert?	3
2. What is Social Anxiety?	14
3. Social Anxiety, Self-Esteem, and Stress	22

PART II
OVERCOMING SOCIAL ANXIETY AND SHYNESS

4. Overcoming the Stress of Social Anxiety	33
5. Improving Your Self-Esteem	45
6. Taking Charge of Your Life	52
7. Reaching Your Potential	58

PART III
SUCCEEDING AS AN INTROVERT

8. Being an Introvert in an Extroverted World	67
9. Building Confidence	77
Conclusion	87
Let's Soar Together	91
More Information	93
Found a Typo?	95
About the Author	97
Books by Jonathan Green	101
One Last Thing	105

DON'T GO IT ALONE

The hardest part of personal growth is going it alone. When you are in isolation, the night can seem too dark, and success can seem so far away.

We often quit right before we could experience our biggest success. Join something bigger than yourself where you can get the support, feedback, and guidance you need to achieve your desired success.

Please join my FREE, private Facebook group, filled with supportive people on the same path as you!

https://servenomaster.com/community

This is a great place to chat with me daily, share your experiences with the exercises and find a supportive group of people who are all on the same journey as you.

INTRODUCTION

One morning, when I was seven or eight years old, my parents burst into the room with fake smiles on their faces to give me some confusing news. "Jonathan!" they said, "We have got some great news! We have found a new friend for you. We found you an amazing therapist named Sam."

Those simple words kicked off a journey of discovery of my many flaws, including my social anxiety, my shyness, my awkwardness, my fear of interacting with people in public, and my inability to communicate with people effectively.

Like many modern parents, their first thought when their child had a problem was to turn to the medical-industrial complex. Got a problem? Get a doctor, get a pill, get an injection. This was not the first time my parents turned to a mental health professional to fix me, and it would not be the last, either.

If you have read my book, *Overcoming Depression*, you know some of my journey through psychologists, shrinks, and counselors. A big part of my problem was depression, but another part was the challenge that interacting with people represented for me. My natural introversion was apparent, and when your parents think that something is wrong with you, you begin to wonder if they're right.

I grew up watching a lot of afterschool specials and Lifetime movies about kids with weird problems – like the kid who was a psychopath but did not know it – and I began to wonder if there was something wrong with me to such an extent that I was unable to perceive it.

Did I have a problem within my psyche that I could not see?

In many of those movies where the main character has a mental problem, whether it is insanity, psychosis, or some other intense mental disease, the subject is never aware of it. The person is hearing voices, but to them, the voices are real. Was there something so dramatically wrong with me that I could not even see it? Was I this far gone down the path?

Social anxiety can be very stressful. There are certain public situations that can become overwhelming, and I still find certain social situations overwhelming – my heart starts racing, my palms get sweaty, and I cannot hold it together. My breath starts changing, and I wonder if I am going to pass out from nervousness.

I have struggled with various forms of social anxiety for my entire life, and I have stared that monster in the eye. Just because the people around you might not understand it, it does not mean that your social anxiety is not real.

There is nothing wrong with being introverted, and there is nothing wrong with being shy or quiet. When our parents are faced with an unknown situation, they start throwing around labels and terms – like someone lost, reaching for a light switch in the darkness.

Any term can feel better than a situation you don't

understand. When you're smart and reserved, your parents might call you "cerebral." But if you were to ask them the definition of that word, they wouldn't be quite sure.

It's not malicious on their part. This is how many people cope with confusing situations. You can't fix a problem until you have a name for it.

A large percentage of our population is introverted. One of the most common psychological tests is called the Myers-Briggs test. It measures personalities along four spectrums, the first of which is the range from introverted to extroverted.

If the first measure on one of the most common psychological profiling tests in the world is how introverted you are, then there must be a lot of introverts out there! You are hardly alone.

I sat down to write this book for a singular reason. This is the book that I wish my parents had given me when I was younger, instead of trying to "fix" me by spending massive amounts of money on "professionals" and filling out loads of insurance forms. Those things never worked for me.

In America, there are more people on prescription medications than there are people.[1] If you look at the top ten mental health diseases, there are enough prescriptions out there to prescribe every single person in America one and a half times.[2]

I doubt that every single person in our entire country suffers from a mental disease that requires powerful chemicals to be dumped into their bloodstreams, but it's all about repeat business for pharmaceutical companies.

One in ten men and one in five women take a mental health medication daily.[3] Do you really think that 20 percent of the population needs to be medicated that much?

When you go to a mental health professional, all they

are thinking about is getting you back in there. What is the first thing any psychologist or therapist says to you? "I need to see you two or three times a week." Once a week only if you are lucky. Some people go there five times a week, and with the cost of therapy between one and five hundred dollars an hour, that is thousands of dollars a week.

None of these methods has ever worked for me, but I can only speak through my experience, and I have never had a good experience with counselors, therapists, and psychologists. None of them was ever able to help me; all they ever talked about was how often I needed to come back.

This is a world that certainly favors the extroverted, and as an introvert, you might feel like you are at a disadvantage. But you don't need to spend massive amounts of money or feel like there is something wrong with you. This book is a guide to help you understand who you are and how you can find the advantage in your natural personality traits.

I am still naturally very introverted; I live on an island in the middle of nowhere, and on average, I speak to less than five people who are not family members every week. I often go weeks without speaking to someone outside of my family. I know what it's like to be introverted, but I have also found success in this life.

Together, we are going to build your confidence, overcome your social anxiety and discover how you can survive and thrive in this extroverted world. You are an amazing person; it is time for you to release that amazing into the world without any regrets or wondering if there is something wrong with you.

Together, we are going to find the path for you to express yourself in public without feeling awkward or uncomfortable ever again.

[1] www.cdc.gov/nchs/fastats/drug-use-therapeutic.htm.
[2] www.statista.com/statistics/261303/total-number-of-retail-prescriptions-filled-annually-in-the-us/.
[3] www.psychcentral.com/blog/top-25-psychiatric-medications-for-2016/.

PART I
EXPLORING SHYNESS AND SOCIAL ANXIETY

1

ARE YOU AN INTROVERT?

"Aren't you having fun? Why are you not talking? Are you just shy? What is wrong with you? Do you think you are better than me?" If you are an introverted person who always thinks before speaking, you have probably heard these phrases more than a few times. People misinterpret your quietness or shyness as aloofness and pretentiousness.

When you are different, people do not know what to do and often react in a negative way. That's how we can end up trapped. There are plenty of people who have completely misinterpreted my inner dialogue and my personality simply because I was not talking as much as them.

There is that old adage "If you have nothing nice to say, do not say anything at all." If I didn't have anything to say, then sometimes I wouldn't say anything. When you are an introvert, you think before you speak, and people who speak before they think do not know how to deal with that. It can feel overwhelming and a little bit uncomfortable.

As you have decided to grab this book, you could be anywhere on the spectrum of shyness, social anxiety, and social awkwardness. Maybe public speaking makes you sweat, or maybe you are just uncomfortable talking to the opposite sex. Maybe you have trouble making friends, or you just feel like you never know what the right thing to say is when you are with a group of people.

If you feel frustrated in any way with your shyness, don't worry; there are some great advantages to being an introvert, and we are going to dive into that as we work through this process. By the time we finish, you are going to feel empowered rather than hindered by social anxiety.

If you are introverted like me, you are probably sick of people constantly accusing you of being shy, aloof or any other random label they attach to you. The reality is, it is not always the person; it is often the situation. When you are around strangers in certain types of environments or social situations, that is when you get quiet. When you are in unfamiliar territory, you do not say anything.

But when you are around your friends and people who you are comfortable with, when you are in a situation where you feel like you know what to do, then you are very comfortable opening up, speaking out, telling jokes and connecting with the people around you.

If you are still in school, you may not know what to say in the halls, but when you are in the classroom, you feel comfortable raising your hand and giving the answer because you understand school, even if you do not understand the other students.

Introverts are just as creative, smart, dynamic, intelligent, and funny as extroverts. It is just that we express ourselves in a slightly different way. We prefer smaller groups. We prefer depth of friendship to breadth of friendship. I don't need five hundred shallow friends from Facebook; I would rather have five close real-world friends I connect with in a meaningful way.

Unfortunately, the West is dominated by extroverts; introverts do not often become the president or a CEO. In a world where extroverts dominate, we have got to stick together. We have been marginalized and stigmatized for too long, and there are too many misconceptions about us. In the West, the introvert is labeled and dismissed, and this can make it difficult for us to compete and interact in school and the workplace.

I know you are a deep thinker. I am too, and that is why I have worked so hard in putting together these tools to help you achieve the same success in life that I have. I will help you unlock your full and unbelievable potential.

The Spectrum

Introversion and extraversion are measured on a continuum. There is no such thing as a person who is one hundred percent extroverted or one hundred percent introverted. If you were one hundred percent introverted, you would have a different problem; you would never speak to anyone ever, and that is an entirely different medical problem beyond the scope of this book.

Most likely, you are comfortable with being extroverted in some situations but not most situations. My personality is quite binary in that if I need to be extroverted for a short amount of time, I can.

In my business books, I talk about how I travel two to three times a year to conferences.

I like conferences that last three days. Any longer than that and my ability to be an extrovert starts to fade. If you see me at one of these events, I am the life of the party. You would assume I'm deep at the extrovert end of the spectrum. But you would be wrong. It takes months of introvert time for me to save up enough energy to spend seventy-two hours talking to strangers.

The second I say goodbye at the conference, my extrovert side shuts down. I am silent in the taxi on the way to the airport, and I don't say one word to the person next to me on the airplane. I will spend the next six months on my tropical island, avoiding strangers like the plague.

If you saw me at a conference and then at home, you would not believe that I am the same person.

My wife is my translator to the world. She handles the majority of my communications with strangers when we are at home. Not because she speaks the local language, which she does, but because I prefer to avoid those interactions.

She is the one who talks to the mailman, the doctors, and our children's teachers. When I found my true love, my first thought was, "Ah, finally someone who can talk to all of the people I do not want to talk to anymore." Conversations that are not a big deal to anyone else, I would rather just not have. If I do not have anything to say to someone, I don't really want to talk to them.

Yet when you see me at a conference, you would never believe that I am an introvert.

You can find where you are on the spectrum. Maybe you are like me, someone who can turn it on or off for short amounts of time. I need those six months of introversion to recharge for the next time I need to be outgoing.

Most people lean primarily towards one end or the other. Most of the time, they are either quiet or loud. Some people can straddle the fence and be loud half the time and quiet half the time, but those people are an exception. We want to discover where you are on the extrovert-introvert spectrum. Here are a couple of signs that you are hanging out at the introvert end of the spectrum just like me.

Signs You are an Introvert

1. **We generally need more time alone**, and we use this time to recharge and build up our energy. We are more sensitive and become overstimulated more easily than extroverts. Being stuck in extended social situations becomes overwhelming. You might be okay spending two hours at a work function, but the thought of doing a three-day weekend or one of those team-building exercises fills you with dread. That is certainly how I feel.

2. **We think first and act later.** We are less likely to be high-risk-takers. Extroverts tend to take action and then look at the consequences of their action; this is why they end up in trouble more often than introverts. They make more poor decisions than they would if they had just spent a few minutes thinking before speaking or taking action.

3. **We are excellent observers and listeners.** Extroverts spend most of the time talking, and when they are not talking, they are just waiting for their turn to start talking again. As introverts, we want as much information as possible before making decisions, and we are happy to let other people do all of the talking.

People often misinterpret my quietness for weakness, so they spend a long time talking and revealing useful things about themselves in a social competition, not realizing that I am using all of that time to analyze and understand them and wait for my opportunity.

I am not a loud, confident person. My confidence does not express itself through rashness, shouting, or physical domination. You will never see me do any of those things because I find them unnecessary. My confidence is quiet; I do not need other people to know what I am capable of because I already know. You have that within yourself as well, as a confident introvert.

4. We have a strong sense of self-awareness. We have a strong thought life and can understand our feelings and express a wide spectrum of emotions. The more time you spend analyzing your emotions, the more aware you become of the wide spectrum of emotions that we can experience. An extrovert would say, "These introverts are really good at feeling; I am too busy living." That is fine; there is nothing wrong with being an extrovert. It is just a different way of experiencing the world.

5. We hate getting trapped in small talk; we would much rather engage in deep ideas. This is the reason I do not often talk to strangers. When I talk to other people on my island, we do not have many things in common. We can talk about the ocean or the weather, but those topics are very shallow, and it is always the same conversation.

I would much rather go deep with someone who is writing a book or has a passion that dovetails with mine. I do not like having short conversations. It does not interest me, and that is the difference between the shotgun and the sniper rifle.

The shotgun shoots hundreds of tiny pellets – a little conversation with everyone around you. You try to have as many social media friends as possible, whereas the sniper would rather have one conversation that lasts all night and is very meaningful.

6. We tend to be better abstract thinkers and deep thinkers. Now it almost sounds like we are bragging. Think about it though; we spend more time thinking, so of course, we are better at it.

I can tell because of my creative side and my writing skills, where I create a world from my imagination. I do all of my work by myself – just a piece of paper and my imagination.

7. We tend to be good at learning by observation. When I began writing my first book ten years ago, I was single, and I wanted to learn how to talk to women. I was very shy and socially awkward, and perhaps that feeling resonates with you.

I would go into a bar and just watch everyone because I wanted to understand the system. I eventually became good at dating because I had a great understanding of social interactions.

I could walk into a room and understand what people were doing that most of the other people don't see. If you are in a bar, and a man and a woman walk in together, the automatic assumption is that they are a couple. Most of the time that is right, but not always. Many times, it's a brother and a sister, co-workers, or just a couple of platonic friends.

Extroverts miss that because they are caught up in their assumptions.

When you spend more time analyzing and just watching, you start to *see* things. I became a person who waited for opportunity. My first ability was not thinking of brilliant words to say; it was waiting for the right moment. Part of my great skill in dating was my ability to be completely invisible. I could stand in a bar filled with beautiful men and women, and I did not exist until I opened my mouth.

Understanding when it is the right moment can help us introverts overcome our fear.

The Stacked Deck

In our society, introverts are the outliers – we are perceived as an exception, while extroverts are considered "the norm." It can be hard, living in a society that measures us by how outgoing we are when that is not our natural state. We are caught between the desire to be who we are and the desire to be who everyone else wants us to be.

That is the tug-of-war you may feel every single day.

Extroverts grow up in a culture where their personality is constantly affirmed. It starts in school, where extroverted kids get the most attention from the teachers, are the most popular and get to date the prettiest people. It is the extroverted people who get the rewards early on in life. Introverts have to wait a little bit longer for those good times to start rolling.

Extroverts do not understand it, so they do not even think about it. Society favors them, and they are the majority, so they do not understand that there is nothing wrong with us; we just experience the world in a different way. You are unlikely to get any sense of compassion, interest, or curiosity about your difference from an extrovert; they just will not understand it.

You do not need to develop an inferiority complex or to start thinking that there is something wrong with you, because there is not. As introverts, we tend to avoid confrontation.

When you combine our natural aversion to confrontation with lower confidence levels, which result from feeling like you don't fit in and constantly having your personality questioned, you can become a person who doesn't stand up for yourself, even when you should.

Do not let anyone make you feel like there is something wrong with your emotions. Of course, you do not want to let your emotions control you and be a slave to your emotions, but your emotions can certainly color how you view the world. Nevertheless, you do not need to let the rest of the world walk all over you. It is fine to pick and choose your battles.

Even now, when I enter a negotiation in my personal life, people sometimes try to walk all over me because they misinterpreted my quietness and slow negotiating for weakness. In my business life, people know better. I have been running my own company for a very long time, and I never enter a negotiation unless I am ready to walk away when I do not get what I want.

Just because we are quiet does not mean that we are weak. As we build your confidence, you will unlock the powers within you to handle negotiations and to keep people from walking all over you. You will become stronger and get the life you deserve.

Assessment

If you are still unsure of whether you are an introvert, extrovert, or where you fall on the spectrum, that is okay. I put together this quick assessment to help you find out exactly where you are on the spectrum. For each question, choose just one answer. At the end of the test, you will find a scoring key. Have fun!

1. After a long day at work with lots of meetings, what would you most enjoy as a way to unwind?

    a) Going to the pub or to a fun get-together with co-workers.

    b) Spending some quiet time at home, alone, watching a great movie and eating your favorite food.

2. Which of these occupations would you prefer?
    a) Professional public speaker.
    b) Novelist.

3. Would you describe yourself as outgoing?
    a) Yes.
    b) No, or not usually.

4. You are at a party. What are you most likely to be doing?

    a) Freely moving from group to group, effortlessly taking part in small talk and introductions.

    b) Talking with one or two close friends.

5. How often do you feel the need to be alone?
   a) Rarely, or never.
   b) I frequently feel the need to be alone, especially after spending a lot of time in any kind of social situation.

6. Which of these do you usually prefer?
   a) Fun and lively small talk.
   b) A deep or philosophical conversation.

THE MORE A) ANSWERS YOU CHOSE, the more extroverted you are. The more b) answers you chose, the more introverted you are. If the majority of your answers were b), then it's time to celebrate, because you are probably an introvert, and you are about to learn about how to show the world how wonderful you really are!

2

WHAT IS SOCIAL ANXIETY?

Do you feel nervous before or during social events? How severe is this anxiety or nervousness? Have other people noticed this nervousness or anxiety within you?

Social anxiety is a sense of nervousness, worry, or even fear that arises before or during social situations. It has to do with interacting with other people, and it arises from the fear that we might embarrass ourselves, or that people will think badly of us.[4] There is often no rational reason to support this fear; we are just afraid that something bad is going to happen.

Introverts can find social situations emotionally draining. We recharge our batteries when we are by ourselves. Solitude gives us time to process our emotions and feelings after interacting with others.

We need to be by ourselves to recharge, and solitude is where we gain our strength. Without that time to process our emotions, or when we are forced to stay in long social situations, we begin to run out of energy and become more awkward, uncomfortable, or even unpleasant.

In between spending time with other people, I need time by myself in order to recharge my batteries and feel comfortable in social situations. This feeling is not relegated just to strangers. I feel this way even with my family, my children, and my wife, whom I absolutely love. This does not mean I don't love my family. It's just the way my genetics work; my psychological make-up requires solo time so I can enjoy the time with them all the more.

It can be overwhelming when an introvert is forced to spend too much time in a social situation. Without enough time to process our emotions, they start to back up until they overflow, and it feels like the emotion factory is going to explode.

The way we process emotions requires that time afterward, and this is actually the same way that people fall in love.

We do not fall in love when we are with the other person; we fall in love when we are apart from them.

When you are with someone you're attracted to, it is hard to think about anything else. Your emotions and physical desires are controlling the system. When you're by yourself, and you still miss that person and think about them, that's when you know that feeling is something more than lust.

Without that processing time, it is very difficult for something to happen.

This is why people who spend a lot of time together early in the relationship have hot but short relationships.[5] The relationship burns brightly, but then they quickly fall out of love with each other because they had no time for the love to solidify. Emotions that are not properly processed never transition from short into long-term emotional memory.

People who suffer from social anxiety are often called shy. "Shy" is a very powerful word, and sometimes, it is also one of the most horrible things you can say about a person. It is a way we can control other people and limit them.

When you are labeled as shy, people will see you through the lens of shyness and think, "Oh wow, he is doing so good for a shy guy," or, "That is an interesting thing to say for a shy person." It becomes an albatross around your neck, weighing you down and limiting you. When people call you shy, it is not a compliment or just an adjective; it is a curse.

Very often, the person saying it and the person hearing it have two different definitions of the word "shy." We can call someone shy because they do not speak in social situations when they are actually mute. Until you find that out, you could easily think, "Oh, they are so shy they are not talking at all."

Maybe they have a different type of social anxiety disorder. You could easily mistake someone's autism or Asperger's for shyness, when in fact, they have a medical condition that is very different.

Even worse, we sometimes misinterpret shyness for aloofness. "She doesn't talk to us because she thinks she is better than us."

No one ever says, "I want to be friends with someone shy", or, "I just wish I were shy." It is not something to strive for. It is not something that is desirable, and therefore it is a negative. When someone calls you shy, they are belittling your experience of the world.

As someone who suffers from a degree of social anxiety, I would rather not be called shy. It is such a broad term that it becomes meaningless. All it really means is that I am less – there is something missing in me.

When your social anxiety is so severe that it affects your daily life, it is possible you suffer from a diagnosable condition called "social anxiety disorder," also known as "social phobia."[6] Your social anxiety is so severe it becomes a barrier on your existence. People who suffer from this form of anxiety have an intense and overwhelming fear of being watched and negatively judged by others.

Even if you suffer from an extreme form of social anxiety disorder, you can be very aware that logically there is no rational reason for these thoughts. We know that everyone is selfish. Everyone's favorite topic is themselves, because all humans are narcissists, no matter what we say.

Yet we sometimes forget that other people are selfish, too. We can become totally self-absorbed and think that we are the center of the universe and that other people are just focusing on us. But in fact, everyone is focusing on themselves.

It's easy to think that 200 people at that high school dance are all focused on you, but if there is one thing we know about teenagers it's that they are all self-absorbed. Every single one of those people is only thinking about themselves. The lies social anxiety feeds us are the opposite of reality, but no one said social anxiety disorder was rational.

When you have an extreme version of social anxiety disorder, it can lead to panic attacks before or during social situations. You can even have a panic attack at the very thought of talking to someone, or maybe a panic attack strikes as soon as you say hello to a person.

A panic attack[7] can cause rapid, difficult breathing and chest pains, and you may feel disoriented or weak. Some people feel a numbness or a tingling sensation in their fingers and hands and unexplained sweating and chills. When you have these physical manifestations, your anxiety becomes even stronger – it becomes a border.

If you get nervous and have a panic attack one out of every ten times you go to the grocery store, you will stop going to the grocery store. This is negative reinforcement, and it keeps you living in fear that things will always end horribly.

Your universe ends up getting smaller and smaller until you get trapped in your house or even in one room in your house. As we push back against your social anxiety and work our way through the exercises, techniques, and activities in this book together, you will notice your universe getting larger. Your borders will expand rather than shrink.

Reflection Questions

I recommend that you keep a Stop Shyness and Social Anxiety Journal. This is a journal where you can write down your answers and experiences throughout this book. Keeping a journal is very important because it gives you a reliable record of where you are coming from and where you are going.

I have created a companion Social Anxiety Journal to this book that you can buy, but you can also just buy a notebook at the store. My Journal has a little more structure and organization, but this book has all of the tools you need so do not feel obligated to buy anything else. But it is there if you like a more organized resource.

In your Social Anxiety Journal, please write down your answers to the questions below. It is very important to go beyond just reading these questions and answering them in your mind. If you want to see success by the time you get to the end of this book, writing down your answers to these questions and taking part in the activities is critical. If you just read this book and do not do any of the activities or answer any questions, the book will probably not work.

Social anxiety is the fear of interacting with other people. If you will not even interact with this book, you are never going to get to where you deserve to be. If you just trust me and come along with me on this journey, I promise you we are going to make a difference, and you are going to see some amazing results.

However you choose to track your progress, please write down your answers to the following questions:

1. Based on what you have read, do you think you might have social anxiety? On a scale of 1 to 10, where do you see yourself on the social anxiety disorder spectrum? A 0 or 1 means that you are comfortable talking to other people, while a 10 means that you cannot even leave your house or your room. Where are you on this spectrum?

2. Do you experience anxiety or fear during and/or before social situations? How intense is that fear?

3. Does the fear of social situations interfere with your life? If it does, how severely and in what ways do you feel that social anxiety has affected your life?

4. What steps are you going to take to deal with the problem?

Social Anxiety Borders Activity

Anxieties, fears, and phobias limit our universe. The things we are afraid of cause us to avoid specific situations. We are going to find the borders of your universe. At this stage, our goal is not to take you beyond your comfort zone. The goal here is just to find its exact limits.

In your Journal, make a list of every social situation you are afraid of. Whether it is going to a meeting, speaking in public, meeting strangers, eating in public, going to a job interview, or just talking to someone of the opposite sex, list as many specific situations as you can. Once you have that list, we are going to spend the next week digging in and seeing exactly where your border is.

Let's say you have "job interviews" on your list. Here is the process of going to a job interview: you go online, see what jobs are available, and send in your application and resume for jobs that might be relevant. They respond to you and give you a time to show up, and you confirm that you are going to the interview. You get dressed, get to the interview location and wait for your turn to be called. Then you go into the room, you answer their questions and ask your own questions.

We want to find out where along that path your moment of fear is. Your border might be so far back in the process that you cannot even contemplate the idea of looking at jobs on a website. If you cannot even look online without freaking out, then write that down.

First, we want to establish a deep understanding of your fear. If you wrote down public speaking, find an event like an open mic night, a poetry night, or Toastmasters meeting where you have to talk to strangers and speak. Just see how far you can go. Maybe you can find the event but you cannot sign up for it, or maybe you can sign up but you do not go. Maybe you do go, but you don't want to talk and you just listen, and that is your border.

If your real area of social anxiety is talking to the opposite sex, go to a bar or put yourself in a situation where you have to talk to someone and see how far you can go. Can you go to the bar and look at someone? Does that get you nervous? Can you make eye contact but you would never go and talk to them? If they come and talk to you, can you continue the conversation or is that where you stop?

For each of your different areas of social anxiety, find your border. Rather than just writing down where you think your border is though, go and try to reach that border. I am not going to ask you to cross it, but to make sure you know exactly where it is. You might be able to go beyond what you thought was your border.

For many of us, these borders have existed for years or even decades, and we would not have even noticed if it changed. Perhaps your border has gotten closer or further away without you noticing.

I know this activity might make you a little bit nervous, but remember that the moment you start to feel uncomfortable, you just stop and write it down. We are just trying to find where the border is, and when you have completed this activity, I will be waiting for you in the next chapter.

4   www.socialphobia.org/social-anxiety-disorder-definition-symptoms-treatment-therapy-medications-insight-prognosis.

5   www.psychologytoday.com/intl/blog/meet-catch-and-keep/201406/how-much-time-should-couples-spend-together.

6   www.adaa.org/understanding-anxiety/social-anxiety-disorder.

7   www.adaa.org/understanding-anxiety/panic-disorder-agoraphobia/symptoms.

3

SOCIAL ANXIETY, SELF-ESTEEM, AND STRESS

If you have problems with social anxiety, you know already that it can affect your confidence, self-esteem, and how you view yourself. Sometimes you can sit there thinking, "Why can't I do this? What is wrong with me? Why am I not normal?"

It becomes an intense internal stress, where we are caught between who we are and who we wish we were, and we cannot figure out what is wrong with us. It is sometimes hard to express what you are going through, and it is a bit of a catch-22.

Your problem is that you cannot talk to other people because you feel uncomfortable, and the only way to deal with your problem is to talk with other people; you are trapped. The solution is the problem, and the problem is the solution.

We know that our social anxiety is not logical, and while it might seem helpful to view it this way, it actually leads to more problems because every time we look at our issue we have a sense of guilt or failure. This sense of disappointment can push you into a negative cycle, where every time you try and fail, you feel a little bit worse. This is one of the reasons that we stop trying.

Who wants to feel worse each time they try and fail?

This stress begins to push more and more downward pressure on your self-esteem. You want to feel good about yourself, and you would have confidence in yourself, but you cannot do things that other people do. You feel limited, and you are caught in a cycle.

The good news is that the same aspect of your personality that creates this problem is going to help you break out. Remember: as introverts, we have a greater sense of self-awareness. We can use that ability to analyze, understand, and reverse our problem.

You have a strong capacity for introspection and reflection, and the first step on the path to healing is to diagnose the problem. The second step is to be aware each time the problem triggers. You have a solid understanding now of exactly where each of your barriers is and what your triggers are.

Now that we know what causes your social anxiety, we can deal with each of your triggers exactly where they are, and your deep sense of self-awareness is a major advantage in this battle.

Being an Introvert is Great

We have already covered the negative consequences that an introvert can face in our society. It's time to dial into ten of the most amazing aspects of being introverted and why you have a major advantage in life! Once we overcome the small social anxiety hump, you are going to become limitless.

1. Introspective ability and self-awareness. The ability to self-diagnose is something that often has to be taught, but because you are self-aware by nature, you will master this step far quicker than anyone else. Your introspective ability and self-awareness will help you improve and go through each of your personal development cycles much more quickly than the extroverts out there.

2. Deep thinkers are very creative. As an introvert, you already know that you are also a deep thinker. You have an innate ability to look at things in a philosophical, artistic, and logical way and see multiple aspects and dimensions of the same idea. Introverts are often the most creative of people, and we express our creativity in different ways – from art to poetry or even designing video games and creating apps.

3. You have strong focus. You are able to stay on task for longer than most other people, and your ability to work without distraction is what separates you from the crowd.

People are often amazed by how many books I write, how many words I can write per day, and the amount of time I can put into a project. Even before my eyes started to fail me, I was writing 20,000 words a day.

Most other authors are targeting 1,000 to 2,000. I was ten to twenty times more productive than the competition. Not because I am a better writer, but because I can sit for hours and just type away.

This requires a strong ability to focus, and the best part is that we enjoy it when we mastering and complete a task.

4. You have an independent spirit. We are not afraid to live life on our own terms and think outside of the box. In our society, we are not like the majority of the population, and we do not see the world the same way everyone else does. What we want to do is not what everyone else wants to do, and we enjoy our solitary and singular activities.

5. You are less impulsive. When I was eight years old, at summer camp, the other kids used to call me "Judge Green" because I was always worried about the rules. I was not as impulsive as the other kids. I was the one who always thought that we should all have life jackets on a boat, and of course, the kids were laughing at me, "We don't need life jackets. Nothing bad is going to happen!"

They saw the world in a different way and didn't think twice before doing something silly or reckless. Our ability to find wisdom even at an earlier age is what makes us excellent leaders. Not only do we see the dangers, but we also know when it is the right time to make the move. Anyone can take risks, but as introverts, we are excellent at taking calculated, intelligent risks.

6. You have a greater capacity to be a visionary. All that introspection and internal dialogue within your head gives you the ability to create a universe and imagine the world the way you want it to be. This is how you can bring people into alignment. When people see that great vision, which extroverts struggle to create, they get pulled into it. This is how you can become a leader of an army of extroverts.

7. You take part in deep and meaningful conversations. When I was younger, I often struggled to communicate with the people around me, as I would try to explain my argument, and they simply could not grasp it or get left far behind. You have the ability to see deeper arguments and take your exchanges and conversations a step further. You do not waste your time on small talk; you see conversation as valuable. You are focused on quality rather than quantity.

8. You are better at influence and persuasion than you think. When people think of influence and persuasion, they usually think of a loud and self-confident person who can get people to do what he or she wants through some form of pressure or even intimidation. That is a lower level or persuasion. True influence and persuasion is where someone does what you want them to do and think it was *their* idea. Unlike extroverts, we can be subtle.

9. You are an excellent listener and observer. I cannot tell you how many times I have watched people make a horrible decision just because they did not wait long enough.

A few years ago, before I met my wife, when I was in my wild late twenties, I would go out to a bar with my friends with the intention of talking to a woman. My friends would try to talk to every single woman the second she walked in. They did not want to miss a single opportunity, and they used the "shotgun approach."

They were convinced that if they talked to enough women, eventually, one would fall for his charms.

I am sure you are familiar with this approach because it is very common, and it does work for many people.

As I grew my confidence and became more comfortable with who I am, I became a man of great patience, and I saw myself more as a "trapper" – someone who waits for the right moment. I would only talk to one woman on a night because I spent a lot of time studying, listening, and observing people until the opportunity was there.

There are millions of reasons why an interaction with another person can fail. You can walk up right in the middle of someone else's conversation, or when someone gets a bad text, or right when they are about to go to the bathroom. Any of those things will destroy your chances, and none of them is your fault.

I like to take my time and see how people interact with each other, how the room is working, and this carries on very much into my business interactions. I like to observe how people treat each other before they know who I am. My ability to go unnoticed allows me to see how people act and talk before they realize I am there.

10. You are excellent at written and detailed communication. We are not the best at verbal communication, that is an extrovert's talent, but there is something about the written word that we're just a little more comfortable with.

One of my greatest challenges is that I cannot write by hand anymore. I have a medical problem with my eyes that limits what I can do with computers, so I have to write my books by dictation, and this alters my voice. When I edit my books, there is a part of me that wants to rewrite every sentence to make it more eloquent – to unleash that part of me.

You, as an introvert, have a natural ability to be a great

poet or writer, so you should definitely consider writing a few words and seeing what you are capable of.

What Does It All Mean?

You are probably asking yourself, "How do I put this all to work? What do all of these introvert advantages have to do with my social anxiety, stress, and self-esteem cycle?" Don't worry, this book is going somewhere. There is a destination.

By the end of the next few chapters, you are going to feel more equipped and have more tools in place. If you stay the course and do all the activities, it will all become clear.

As introverts, we are comfortable spending time with ourselves. We are going to use that time more effectively to reflect on your strengths and think of ways to build your confidence. We are also going to develop some strategies for dealing with the obstacles you might face.

Reflection Questions

In your Journal, please answer the following questions:

1. Has social anxiety affected your stress levels and self-esteem? If so, in what ways has it affected you?

2. Were you more confident when you were younger? Think about your first day of school. How did you view the world? For me, I was excited; there was no fear. Social anxiety had not yet entered my life. Take some time to remember and write down those feelings – those moments in your past where all you felt was excitement about the future.

3. Do you feel your struggle with social anxiety has given you insights that those who have not dealt with it lack?

Activity

We are going to try something that is going to take you a little bit outside of your comfort zone, but hopefully not too much. We do not want to blast through your barriers; we just want to push against them a little bit.

Choose one or even a few of your barriers. Imagine you are that five-year-old version of yourself, or any past version of yourself – just choose a moment from your past from your answer to the second reflection question in this chapter. Pretend to be that person as you go out and push yourself against that barrier.

To implement this activity successfully, first of all, you have to remove expectation, and secondly, you have to remove social consequences. Allow me to give you a few different examples.

Let us say your great fear is talking to people of the opposite gender. You can put yourself in situations where that has to happen but there are no social consequences and there is no expectation. For example, when you go out to meet other people, your intention is to take someone home or get their phone number. If you take that stressor off the table, the only thing you can do is have an enjoyable conversation. Now you are not trying to strive toward some external or faraway goal. Your only goal is to talk to people and have a good time.

Taking away social consequences means you do not do this in a place where people know you.

That way, whatever happens, no one will ever hear about it. Go to a faraway bar or speed-dating event where no one knows you. If you want to get good at giving public speeches or stand-up comedy, do not go to the jam at your local coffee shop the first time you want to give it a try.

It's time for you to go out there, implement this activity, and build on what you did last week. Push the borders a little bit, with that innocence of youth, and then join me in the next chapter.

PART II
OVERCOMING SOCIAL ANXIETY AND SHYNESS

4

OVERCOMING THE STRESS OF SOCIAL ANXIETY

When we look at our social anxiety, it can feel like a mountain. The problem feels insurmountable when we think of it as a single, big challenge. However, breaking down that challenge into smaller pieces turns that mountain from impossible to possible.

Together we are going to break that mountain down into small pieces that we will then focus on one by one. By focusing on one small challenge at a time, the impossible becomes inevitable.

We want to begin by looking at the stress that comes from social anxiety. This is our physical reaction to how social anxiety and shyness make us feel in public situations. If we can overcome that feeling in our body that holds us back, we can start to make a difference.

THERE ARE eleven strategies you can implement to push back this type of stress:

1. **Exercise more frequently.** An infinite number of studies has shown a direct correlation between increased exercise and decreased stress levels.[8] We often get caught up in a loop when we are stressed out and have busy lives, saying, "I'm too busy to exercise." But if we were to dedicate a little bit more time to exercising, our levels of stress would go down.

When you exercise, you release endorphins[9] and other beneficial chemicals into your body, while lowering the number of stress chemicals. You begin to feel a sense of relaxation. You can test this by visualizing situations where you feel the most social anxiety and comparing yourself before and after exercising.

Let us say your most stressful situation is asking questions when you are shopping in the store. For two days in a row, go to similar stores with a similar set of questions. The first day, go as you are. The second day, exercise for half an hour first, take a shower and then go to the shop. See if you feel any different.

This is an interactive book, which means you can experiment and find out whether my techniques work very quickly. After you complete this experiment, when you discover that it does work, you will feel even more motivated to get a little exercise every day.

2. **Give yourself time to reflect and challenge negative thoughts.** You are becoming more introspective, and that does not mean quieter. It means you are becoming more aware of your thoughts and the thoughts behind your thoughts – the reasons why we think certain thoughts and why we get caught in certain thought loops.

When you look directly at your fear and understand its

cause, it begins to break apart. You can look at the smaller components and, with logic and understanding, push those thoughts away.

When you feel negative thoughts entering your mind, you can just reject them; you have that option. You can look at that thought and go, "There is no reason for me to think this. Why would I think that?"

3. Think about and solidify your goals. It is worth being very clear about what your desire is. When we create vague goals, we get vague results. Saying "I want less social anxiety" is a pretty meaningless statement. What does that mean? We must be more specific.

When I started out on my journey, every time I discovered a social anxiety wall, I would write down a very specific goal. Knowing your destination will make it easier for you to get there. When we do not have clear goals, we can get knocked off-track quite easily.

This year has been a very tiring year for my family. Every single member of my family has been through a major medical problem. When your wife and kids are sick, it is hard to make time to go to the gym. All you do is work, worry, and do everything you can to make sure that everybody is okay.

When major things happen, they can knock you off-track, but if we write down our goals, we can get back on track more easily after those periods of trauma have passed.

When you write down your goals for overcoming shyness and social anxiety, the solution becomes more visceral. You can see it, you can feel it, and when you achieve it, you will know it. Write down your goals in your Journal, and you can check them off when you achieve them, one by one.

4. Start small. Your first small goal can be to go to a place that makes you a little uncomfortable. You do not have to do anything beyond that. Just being somewhere that makes you uncomfortable creates some agitation within you and starts a little bit of movement.

Then your second goal can be to talk to a waiter, a bartender, or a stranger. Work your way up through small goal after small goal. If you break your massive goal into a thousand tiny goals, victory becomes inevitable.

Each time you achieve something significant, pat yourself on the back. Do not focus on the goals you have not achieved yet; just focus on the next goal you've got ahead of you. It is important that you attach a positive emotion to the act of trying, or you will never succeed.

When people try something, and it does not work out on the first try, they sometimes walk back with their tail between their legs and think, "I failed." Even if they accomplish five out of the seven steps to success, they feel like a failure. If you think that way, what you are doing is providing negative reinforcement. You are teaching your body that when you try, the end result is a bad emotion.

If you try something and fail, that is still a success, because you did more than all the people who do not even try. If you keep trying and pushing yourself, and if you feel good every time you try no matter the result, success becomes inevitable. That is the magic of thinking small.

5. Practice makes perfect. A lot of people would refuse to try something because they think they are not any good at it, but that is a trap of their own making. How do you know that you are not good at something until you try?

If we attach a positive emotion to the act of trying, then we will be consistent in our efforts, and we will enjoy the journey towards success. That is why we do things that make us feel good; we are driven by good emotions and desire to feel good.

If you break down your goal into small pieces and encourage yourself every time you try, each time you achieve a small goal will be a moment of success and a step further towards your destination. If you look at the trees rather than the forest, social stress will diminish, and you will get better and better at whatever you are trying to master.

The more you practice, the more effective these techniques become. The way to get good at job interviews is to go to loads of them. I did not get good at talking to women or business people after five conversations. I have talked to tens of thousands of people, focusing on the process of interactions. That is how I became successful.

6. Find a more social hobby. Depending on where your social barriers are, this might seem very easy or terrifying. Having a social hobby or activity you can participate in, where you are around other people in a low-stress situation, is incredibly beneficial.

I used to go to Meetups, which are local groups you find on meetup.com. One of those I would go to was the Local Entrepreneurs Meetup. It is fascinating. I love to watch people in social situations, and people would come talk to me; I didn't have to do anything.

If you go to these meetings, especially where it is people who are trying to grow their business, they will all talk you in the hopes that they can score you as a client or find some type of economic success.

This is a great place to practice. Sports are another great way of creating environments where you have to be more sociable but it is low-stress, and you are doing something fun. There are loads of hobbies, no matter how small your town or where you live in the world. If you hop on the old Internet, you can do a search for adult sports leagues.

There are ultimate Frisbee teams, adult soccer leagues, and kickball leagues. If you don't want to do something sporty, there are clubs that offer painting, photograph, and all sorts of classes. If you have kids, there are clubs for people who go for walks and jogs pushing a stroller.

There are lots of options, and you just want to pick one that is one step outside of your comfort zone. We do not need to do a huge stretch, but you are not going to overcome your social anxiety unless you are around other people. It does not have to be high-pressure situations. You can do things that you enjoy or things that are fun and good for you.

7. Learn about body language and facial expressions.
When I was around twenty-five, I dated a girl who had a neutral-mean face. This meant that when she was not paying attention, her face looked mean.

Everyone's face has a neutral position. If you are a quiet person, people often mistake you for a jerk or someone who is mean or aloof because you probably have a negative neutral face.

This means that when you're not paying attention, and

your mind starts wandering, you're frowning without even realizing it. This is just enough of a microexpression that is tripping other people's senses, and when they see this, they respond in kind.

You can make a tiny change to your body language and get massive results. People will be friendlier to you, and your mood will improve. You will feel better about yourself.

Many studies show that much of human communication is non-verbal.[10] You can say the friendliest thing in the world, but if your face looks mean, people are going to focus on that meanness. If the way you hold your arms is negative, people are going to respond negatively.

When I wanted to get better at body language, I found an avatar. I found a character on a television show who had the body language I wanted. He was getting the reactions I wanted from people, so I decided to copy that body language. It worked.

Look at yourself in the mirror and imagine that you are somebody else – someone who is just observing you for the first time – and look at how you hold your body. Do you have bad posture? Do you look close off? Do you have a negative face? Do you keep your eyes a little bit squinty? People react to that.

If you clean up your body language, you will notice a lot of results. Good body language and confidence are very powerful and intertwined.

8. Understand and learn to control your body's responses. The more you understand the way your body reacts to situations, the more you can take control.

When I am in a social situation that makes me uncomfortable, my heart starts racing, my breath starts to accelerate, my skin turns a little bit red on my face, and my hands get clammy. I know these responses, and I have a specific way I deal with each of them.

As you learn how your body reacts when you are in uncomfortable situations, you learn which parts you can control and which you cannot. If your hands get sweaty when you are nervous, and you cannot control it, you could wear gloves.

That might be a bit weird in some situations, but handshakes can be a nightmare. One of the things I loved about living in Japan was that I could just bow and never had to shake anyone's hand.

To overcome my racing heart, I have learned to hide all of the other external factors. I cannot control my heartbeat, but I have learned that no one else can feel it, hear it, or detect it, so I do not react to it. I focus more on controlling my breath, so my face does not flush, and thus even when I am absolutely terrified, nobody knows.

It is not that I am never afraid; I have just learned how to hide it and act anyway. That is where you will achieve a great victory. Understand your body and all the little signals that reveal your nervousness. As you make them disappear, this process becomes easier, and it will be easier to interact with other people.

9. Find a cause you believe in and want to work for. We live in a time where people love to virtue signal. This is where people post on Twitter that they believe in a cause, and they feel that posting a tweet is better than taking any action. They do not actually do anything, but they get to feel good about themselves. You can go a step beyond this.

Find a social cause that you believe in and take real

action. Get away from your phone and computer and go out and do something. If you want to help feed the homeless, go work in a soup kitchen once a week.

There are loads of causes and ways you can help people, from passing out blankets after a natural disaster to holding a clipboard at a blood drive. There are lots of things you can do to make a difference and feel good about yourself at the same time. You will be so busy helping people that you won't have time to be nervous.

That is the beauty of a good cause. You are helping other people, but you are also helping yourself. You will be surrounded by other people that are in alignment with you and believe in the same cause as you. Spending time with them will be very casual; you won't be stressed out because you are all focused on the same goal.

10. Focus on the other person. When you are interacting with another person, start to think about their experience. Other people get nervous too. Think about the other person and focus on what is going on in their mind. If you are afraid of the job interview, imagine what it is like having to interview dozens of people, trying to find one person you can connect with.

When you see the world through the other person's eyes, that is empathy. Focus on their experience, and your nervousness will go away. As you get out of your own head and realize other persons are thinking about themselves in that same moment, then you can let go of your fears because you know they are not thinking about you.

Focus on what the other person is saying rather than using the time they are talking as a pause for you to catch your breath before your next comment. If you dig into what they are saying and respond to it, you will find that social interactions are not scary anymore.

11. **Use breathing and muscle relaxation exercises.** Breathing and relaxation exercises have been very effective for me. I use different yoga and meditation exercises throughout the day, and I am constantly bringing them into different parts of my life.

When dealing with a stressful situation, if you have a relaxation technique to help you lower and control your breath, you will find the situation less stressful. This is a powerful way to push back against that anxiety.

When you are focusing on your relaxation technique, it takes up all of your attention, and you do not have bandwidth available for that social anxiety. When you are in that state of relaxation, all of your anxiety stops feeling like a big deal.

Reflection Questions

We have now covered eleven different techniques that you can use to push back against the stress component of social anxiety. Please answer the following questions in your Stop Shyness and Social Anxiety Journal:

1. Have you used any of these techniques before and what were your results?

2. Were any of these techniques surprising or unexpected? Why?

3. Which of these techniques are you most excited to try out next?

4. Do you feel more comfortable about overcoming the

stress component of social anxiety now that you have a toolkit of powerful techniques?

Activity

We have accomplished a lot in this chapter, and there are a couple of approaches you can take for this activity. The first option is to spend the next week implementing as many of these eleven techniques as possible and recording your progress in your Journal.

Write out each time you use one of the techniques and what the result was. Did you find this week more or less stressful than last week? Were you able to push yourself outside your envelope?

You can accelerate this activity by exposing yourself to situations at your social anxiety border and using these techniques to see how much further you can go. Always record your results as fastidiously as possible in your Journal.

Your second option is to find activities and social situations that push you up against that barrier and find a way to make them a consistent part of your life. This means joining a sports league, a Meetup group, or anything that pushes you a little outside of your comfort zone.

You have to be consistent and go every week if you want to see some results in a short amount of time. Don't forget that you can join activities and groups that are not near your home or that you do not really care about, so there is no risk.

I joined that entrepreneurs group because I did not need anything from any of them. I did not need business or clients from them. I just wanted a place to hang out with other entrepreneurs, which meant that if all of them hated me, there would be no long-term consequences; I could just change groups.

[8] www.ajconline.org/article/0002-9149(90)90032-V/fulltext.

[9] www.webmd.com/depression/guide/exercise-depression.

[10] www.psychologytoday.com/us/blog/beyond-words/201109/is-nonverbal-communication-numbers-game.

5

IMPROVING YOUR SELF-ESTEEM

Now that we have taken a deep look at how to deal with the stress of social anxiety, we want to go one step deeper, beyond the reactive and into the proactive. By building up your self-esteem, we can strengthen your defenses and build up a powerful castle around you – a place where you feel safe and secure.

The stronger your sense of belief in yourself, the more you can expand your borders. We are going to work on some very specific tactics and techniques to improve and strengthen your self-esteem, building on the techniques to push back stress from the previous chapter.

There are seven specific techniques that are going to be very powerful for your self-esteem:

1. **Challenge negative thoughts and refuse to be hard on yourself.** This builds on some of our previous work about becoming aware of our thoughts. Whenever you see a negative thought enter your mind, you are going to reject it.

Whenever you catch yourself thinking, "You are not

good enough. You are not pretty enough. You are not smart enough. You will never get this job." You look at thought and go, "No, thanks. I don't need you, and I don't want you. You are not welcome here." You have the power to reject thoughts.

No matter how much our culture likes to pass the buck by blaming our thoughts and emotions as if they were a sentient and separate creature, you control your thoughts; they do not control you. You have the power to reject any thought that you choose. When you have a negative thought, look at it and go, "You are wasting my time, get out!"

2. Learn to recognize your abilities and positive attributes. Your self-esteem may be so battered by your social anxiety that not only can you not leave the house, but you feel like you are not capable of accomplishing anything. I have felt that way myself at times.

We can get so caught up in our negative thought life that we lose control of our self-perception. But if you take the time to assess the good and the bad about you, you will realize there is a lot of good you have not thought about in a long time.

There are a lot of things you have accomplished in your life and a lot of people you have helped in a meaningful way. It can be very helpful to keep a Journal like the one we have been building throughout this book, where you write down every time you accomplish something.

As you begin to track all the good in your life, you will start to notice, "Hey, I am not that bad after all." This will push back those negative thoughts with evidence. When you have opinion in one hand and evidence in the other, the evidence always wins; just ask any judge.

3. Recognize your introversion as a strength! We discussed a host of the advantages of being introverted earlier in this book. One of those is your ability to self-assess and your awareness of your thought life, which is why this process will actually be easier for you.

Remember that quiet does not equal stupid. There are plenty of times when talking is not the right solution. Like the old saying goes, "It is better to be quiet and have people think you are dumb than to open your mouth and prove them right."[11]

We have this false idea in our society that the person talking the loudest is the smartest or the one people fall into alignment with. I can tell you that the highest level of confidence and the leader you want to follow is the one who is quietly confident.

Someone who knows they are right has a significant plan and does not need to shout. Actions speak louder than words, so do not worry about the need to be loud; you simply need to be in alignment with yourself.

4. Recognize the reality of your social anxiety. Anxieties, fears, and phobias dwell in the shadows, but if you take them out into the light and you expose them to the sun, they start to die.

If you reveal to the people around you that you have some social anxiety, they will help you shatter that social anxiety. You have nothing to be ashamed about. Social anxiety is the number one most common anxiety in all of America.[12]

Once you name and face your social anxiety, it is easier to deal with it. You can say to your friends, "I want to do this, but I am nervous," and they will support you. This will make life much easier.

5. Be kind to yourself while going through the process of reducing your social anxiety. This process might take you a while. I know that you hoped you could read this book in an afternoon and your social anxiety would disappear like a snap, and I know that plenty of other books promise that.

I have been through so many of those programs, but they do not work in the long run. Instant solutions fade very quickly. We want something that will last and become a permanent part of your life.

This is a process; give yourself time to accept and absorb that process. Give yourself mercy when you slip up or make mistakes. You can make a problem worse when you notice yourself slipping and then berate yourself for it.

You are on the right path, and as long as you keep trying, that is all that matters. If you let negative thoughts slip in and start to question, doubt or think negatively about yourself, you will break that positive thought loop. Please do not fall into that trap.

6. Be aware of the potential benefits of cognitive behavioral therapy. Cognitive behavioral therapy combines action with therapy, and it is built on many of the concepts we have already covered in this book. You may decide you want to delve a little deeper and get some support from that type of therapist.

Cognitive behavioral therapy is a technique used by psychologist therapists and other mental health professionals to gradually change your thinking and ultimately rewire your brain through a big combination of behavior and cognition. If you are finding this process too hard to go it alone, it is okay to seek help. This form of therapy can be very effective for social anxiety.[13]

7. Get to know other people who are struggling with social anxiety. This is a double-edged sword. If you surround yourself with people who have the same social anxiety as you, it can become a loop where you feed each other and make everyone's social anxiety stronger. I have fallen into this trap before.

I have been in a circle with five or ten other guys who were all nervous about talking to an attractive woman. The nervousness gets stronger and stronger, and you can feel it circling around like a tornado as it goes from person to person. That is the danger of surrounding yourself only with people who have social anxiety.

It can help to get some camaraderie with people on the same journey as you. Having a supportive group and knowing that there are people around you who have been in similar situations is absolutely fine; just be aware of that pitfall.

Reflection Questions

Please answer the following questions in your Stop Shyness and Social Anxiety Journal:

1. Have you used any of the techniques from the previous section before? If so, what were your results?

2. Did you find any of these techniques surprising? If so, why do you think the technique will or won't work?

3. Have you ever made a list of your accomplishments? When was the last time you thought about your greatest accomplishments?

Activity

Make a list of your top accomplishments in life. This list can be ten, twenty, thirty or even fifty things that are special to you or moments in your life where you made a difference. Everyone's list will be different, and it does not matter if you have not saved someone's life or stopped a war. That type of thinking is not allowed here.

Write it down in your Journal or print it out and laminate it, so you can keep it in your wallet. Dedicate enough time to building out your list – don't rush it. You are going to remember moments from childhood and high school that you have not thought about in a very long time.

Every time I use this technique, it reminds me of things I have not thought about in years. Some of my moments are quite significant, and whenever I compare my moments of nervousness to these moments, the nervousness disappears because in moments of great danger, when things were significant, I stepped up.

When my son needed surgery at eighteen months old, I was there for him. I made sure he had the best care possible. He was at the best hospital in the entire country, in the best room, with the best nurses and the best surgeon. Not because I am the best, but because as a father, the best is what I want for my children. It was a scary time for our family, but I stepped up and made things better. Now I can look back on that moment as a time of strength.

Write down your moments of strength and your triumphs. Even if you were just there for someone in your family who was sick, or if you supported someone when they were feeling down, those things really matter.

Look at those moments when you made a difference. Every time you work on remembering this list, you are going to feel good about yourself, and it is going to push your self-esteem up through the roof.

Please work your way through this activity before you start the next chapter.

[11] Derived from Proverbs 17:28.

[12] www.socialanxietyireland.com/social-anxiety/how-common-is-social-anxiety/.

[13] www.psychiatrist.com/JCP/article/Pages/2008/v69n04/v69n0415.aspx.

6

TAKING CHARGE OF YOUR LIFE

Social anxiety can create difficulties in your daily life, including friendships, relationships, and your career. You may have felt these effects yourself. Don't worry! By the end of this chapter, you will know how you can lessen the effects that social anxiety has on your life, and you will know how to make sure that you reach your real potential!

The most important thing to remember here is that starting small is key. Starting small is smart because it will ensure you will never feel overwhelmed and possibly give up. Also, it will give you a regular sense of accomplishment.

Each small step will lead to another one, and before you know it, all of your small steps and accomplishments will have added up to something much larger.

Minimize the Impact of Social Anxiety in your Life

There is no quick fix or panacea solution to overcoming your social anxiety. It is a process, not a moment. If each day we can improve yourself just a little bit, over time, you will see and experience great change. In the short term, we need a few tactics and techniques to help us stay aware of our social anxiety and to deal with the problem directly.

We have looked at confidence, self-esteem, and stress; those are all secondary effects of our core issue. I am going to share with you a few key techniques you can use to push back against that social anxiety directly.

1. **Stay aware.** Whenever you have a moment of social anxiety and you feel stress rising, look your fear in the eye and ask yourself a few critical questions:

- What am I afraid of?
- What is my fear warning me about?
- What is my body protecting me from?
- Is this a real danger?

As I mentioned earlier, the fear of approaching an attractive woman is an atavistic fear that comes from a time when we lived in tribal societies, and if you flirted with the chief's wife or one of the tribal elders, it could you cost your life. You would get bopped on the head with a rock – game over. That fear is no longer necessary in our society. You no longer need that warning.

When you are about to go into the job interview or talk to someone, analyze your fear and ask yourself:

- What exactly am I afraid of?
- How likely is it to happen?
- What will happen if my fear comes true?

Look at how realistic or unrealistic your fear is. Be aware

of it. The more you address your fear directly, the more you break it into component pieces and begin to understand it. You will be able to say to your fear, "You are warning me about this, but that danger is not there anymore. Thank you for that warning, but I am okay."

2. Keep a Journal. We have already begun the process of working your way through a Journal and tracking your efforts. We want to continue that process even after you finish reading this book.

Write down when you have moments of social anxiety and how you deal with them to keep track of your trials and tribulations, your successes and your failures. When you have a success, write it down to remember that moment and commemorate it. When you have a bad day, write that down too so you can remember what went wrong and where you could have done better.

When you track your progress, you can see yourself getting a little better every day, and when you have one of those bad days in a couple of months, you can look back and go, "Wow, my bad day now is what I would have considered a great day six months ago!"

3. Use your strengths. Focus on areas where confidence is strong and look to bring that confidence into areas where your confidence is weak. This is why we discussed finding hobbies and activities that you enjoy so much that the enjoyment overwhelms any social anxiety involved.

Join clubs, societies, sports groups, activities, and classes that sounds fun and exciting to you and will put you in a social environment. You learn something new, you have a fun adventure, and you push against the social borders.

When you are focused on an activity, the more attention and mental bandwidth it takes, the less time you have to experience social anxiety. When you are rounding the bases after a great kick in a game of kickball, you do not have time to think about other people talking to you. You are too busy enjoying your victory.

4. Open up. Social anxiety lives in the shadows. If you tell the people in your life about your social anxiety and explain it to them, they won't belittle you or think less of you. Instead, they will form an alliance with you.

If you are afraid of situation A, and your friend is afraid of situation B, then, as a team, you have nothing to be afraid of because you will take charge whenever you are in situation B, and they can lead in situation A.

Your friends are friends, not enemies. You will discover that once you say your fear out loud, you will begin to take more control of it and diminish the power of that social anxiety.

5. Respect and understand your boundaries. Social anxiety has created boundaries and limits on your life. There are areas where you do not like to go because of the fear that things will go bad. You can live your entire life hiding behind those barriers or you can live a life pushing against those barriers and expanding your territory, which is what we are building in this book.

First, we need to understand those barriers and know the right and the wrong time to push against them. If you push against them every day, it is very stressful, and it can become too much. There is something to be said for exposure therapy but it needs to be controlled.

You want to find the right balance. Once you know where your barrier is, you can spend a lot of time near that barrier without going over until you are strong enough and ready for it.

One of the biggest mistakes a person can make when trying to overcome social anxiety is to do it in a closed social environment. The classic example is the guy who reads a book about how to talk to women and decides to start using those techniques on all of the girls he goes to college with.

No matter the size of your college, the student body is a fixed set; it is a limited social circle. The borders of the college are the number of students that attend there. If you visit a college across town instead, or drive twenty minutes away from where you live and go to bars, clubs, libraries, and coffee shops there, where nobody knows you, you can have as many uncomfortable conversations as needed until you get better. There will be no long-term social consequences.

When you want to push against your barriers – especially when there is a high risk of failure – do it in a no-pressure environment. I am married with three kids, and I have an amazing life even though there are tens of thousands of women who rejected me in the past, and it is fine. It is a learning process. The failures along the way don't matter, only the success at the end.

Respect your borders and only push against them in the right environment.

Reflection Questions

Look at the five techniques in this chapter and all the techniques we have covered so far in this book. It is a lot of information, and it would be impossible for you to try all of these techniques all together. That is not the process; the process is to find the ones that work the best for you.

1. Which techniques do you feel comfortable using?

2. Which techniques can you see working for you and which ones are you willing to try to push yourself outside of your comfort zone?

3. Does learning more techniques make you feel hopeful about the success of this process? Can you begin to imagine what a life without social anxiety would be like?

4. Write a short paragraph describing what your life would be like without any social anxiety. What would it be like to never be afraid again? How would you feel, and what would that person be like? What would your days be like? How would your life be different? How would you actively interact with people differently?

7

REACHING YOUR POTENTIAL

People with social anxiety who are on the introversion spectrum, like I am, have a tendency to fall into a few patterns where we hold ourselves back and limit our own potential.

There are lots of ways in which we end up self-sabotaging or limiting our own success in life. We turn down a job that we do not think we can do. We walk away from a person who is too good-looking for us. We miss opportunities all the time, but we can begin to break the cycle of self-sabotage by being honest about who we are and letting the world know our greatness.

I am a very successful ghostwriter, and I never lack for work. In addition to writing books under my own name, I often help other people write their own books. People often ask me, "How do you become a ghostwriter? How do you find so many clients?" My process is very simple; I tell everyone I know that I am a very good ghostwriter.

That is it. As an introvert, it feels unnatural; it almost feels like I am bragging but it is just honesty. We need to find that balance for ourselves.

1. Let your light shine. It is okay to be honest about what you are good at. It is okay to gauge where you are on the spectrum of success.

Knowing your strengths and weaknesses and being willing to brag in the right way is totally fine. You can let people know you are good at something without shoving it in their faces.

There are people – mostly extroverts at the other end of the spectrum from us – who have a tendency to talk bigger than they are. The fish they caught keeps getting bigger and bigger until it was bigger than the boat they were riding in. These people are making up for a different emotional and psychological challenge that is not the one we have.

You have to find that right calibration where you can talk about what you are good at without making it sound like you think too much of yourself. This is a great experiment you can do outside of your closed social circle.

Practice talking about what you are good at in other environments. As you go through this process and overcome your social anxiety, you will keep recalibrating.

Beginning the process of calibration now will help you and make things easier. Hiding your greatness under a bushel makes people think less of you. When you are nervous about something, it is a red flag. Confidence is magnetic; there is no reason to hide your light.

2. Develop your talents. Remember that you will continue to get better as you grow, learn, and experiment. I am continually learning and growing – in business and in life.

If I did not have to work all the time, I would spend all

my time learning new things – surfing, painting, playing the guitar and teaching my children new skills.

You do not stop learning the moment you turn eighteen. In fact, you *never* stop learning. You continue to grow and as you grow and develop skills in new areas of your life, your confidence grows too, and you become more comfortable with yourself. You will discover that when you talk about and participate in activities where you are confident, your social anxiety fades away.

3. Know that your contribution matters. We often make this mistake where we think that the loudest person is the most important. That is not how successful businesses work. It is not the loudness; it is the effectiveness. Even if you are behind the scenes, your contribution is very significant.

Although I am the face of these books and write them, I have an entire team that helps me go through the process. I have to dictate all my books because of my vision problems. The text then goes through transcription to convert my words into the written word, and then an editor cleans it up and fixes the grammar.

I have several people helping me with each part of the process, and their contributions are significant. They might not be loud, but if they were not part of the squad, the machine would not operate.

You matter; you are significant. If you did not, you would not be there. See the value in your contributions.

4. Move toward success. You can build reward structures so that when you have a moment of success, you can take the time to celebrate it. Look at what you have accomplished. Look at the good things you've done.

We often celebrate massive milestones – we celebrate our birthdays once a year and go on holiday once a year – but you can also have moments throughout the day were you celebrate a success.

Every time you accomplish something, take the time to write it down in your Journal. If it is something big enough, add it to your list of life successes. Keeping track and remembering these moments is significant.

The society we live in makes us believe we have to suffer – the more you suffer along the journey, the better it is. I went through a great deal of struggle as I built my business. I spent a year living in my mother's basement. Then I spent eighteen months living on a couch. That is two and half years of sacrifice.

Does it make my business any better? I don't think so. I wish I could have avoided that pain; I don't think that struggle improves my business in any way. We do not need additional pain because suffering does not improve success. Do not worry about struggling along the journey; things get easier, so just enjoy and reward that!

Reflection Questions

1. Look back on the course of your life and think of the most significant moments. Write down what you think someone who really knows you would say about you if you were gone.

This is an old activity you may have heard of before, where you imagine someone is at your funeral. What would you want your best friend to say? What are the highlights of your life? Take the time to write a few paragraphs and look at the mark you have left on the world. This will help to put your significance in context and realize that you matter. If you are not happy with the results, this will motivate you to change your life.

2. How do you feel about the idea of telling people what you are good at? Does it feel like you're bragging too much? Do you feel like I was bragging too much in that section?

3. How do you respond when you want to find out what someone is good at and they won't tell you?

Activity

In this activity, we are going to practice your calibration. You are going to put yourself into a social situation where you have no consequences – job interviews for jobs you don't want, meetings for hobbies that you have no interest in, classes that you never want to go. You are going to practice telling people what you are good at pushing the envelope to see what is too far and what is not far enough.

The secret to understanding any interaction lies in looking at it from both people's perspectives. When I told you about me being a good ghostwriter, you were looking at it from the outside and not from my perspective. Let us take a moment and look at it as if we were a potential client.

Imagine you are hiring someone to write a memoir for your father. Who would you rather hire and work with – the person who says, "I am pretty good at ghostwriting. I am okay," or the guy who says, "I am a master, and I will honor your father with this memoir; he would be so proud." Of course, you hire the person with more confidence. That is who we are attracted to, and that is how I calibrated myself.

Practice talking about and sharing your greatness, your hobbies, your passions, and the things that interest you. Find out at what point people find you annoying. Find out when you get boring or when people are no longer interested in you.

I learned how to communicate with other people in bars, festivals, and conferences where I knew I would never see those people ever again. You can master your skill and strengthen your personality in environments where there are no social consequences.

PART III
SUCCEEDING AS AN INTROVERT

8
BEING AN INTROVERT IN AN EXTROVERTED WORLD

We live in a world where the majority of the population is extroverted. We often measure ourselves based on a scale from introverted to extroverted, with introverted being a one and extroverted being a ten. Using this scale makes it seem as though being extroverted is best.

Celebrities, people who put themselves out there, and people who make the most noise on social media can often generate a great deal of revenue. We logically assume that this applies across the board, but, in fact, there are many myths about being an introvert. I am going to go through ten of them with you right now. Understanding these myths will help you to break through them.

1. We just don't like being social. This is a common myth sometimes hidden behind just calling us shy. "Shy" is an all-encompassing word that disempowers someone and takes away their sense of control. It is the same thing as calling someone "weak."

Nobody is shy in every situation. We all have different social situations in which we feel comfortable. In general, introverts prefer the depth of a relationship, whereas extroverts prefer breadth.

Extroverts like to have five hundred social media friends, whereas introverts have better interactions with just two or three friends with whom they can have a deep, meaningful relationship. Neither of these is better or worse than the other. They are just different.

Very rarely do I like to be in large social settings, but sometimes I go to large events for work. When I am at these events, I can activate my social energy and connect with a lot of people.

It is not that introverts do not like being social. We just prefer smaller groups.

2. We are boring. Here is another all-encompassing word that is so powerful, hurtful, and limiting. Once someone calls you "boring," anything you say to try to prove otherwise only seems to make it worse. It is a trap from which there seems to be no escape.

When you have social anxiety, you feel uncomfortable in certain social situations, and you do not talk as much. You aren't boring; you are simply waiting for the right opportunity to jump in and speak.

Often, you are surrounded by extroverts who are all fighting over each other for their chance to talk, and you just don't jump in. People who talk too much never learn anything. The only things they ever hear are their own stories. Those are the real boring people.

3. We have nothing interesting to say. The only people who say this are people who don't actually listen. Have you ever met someone who spent the entire interaction talking about themselves? They are the people that go home and think, "Well, everyone else was very boring. He didn't have anything to say."

The reason we didn't say anything is that they never took a breath, gave us the opportunity, or asked a question.

It is not that we don't have anything to say; we just don't say anything when it is unnecessary. We wait for our moment and let other people have their turns. This is simply our approach to social interactions. We are willing to allow the other person to go deep into their stories with the expectation that we will be allowed to go deep next.

4. We are incapable of succeeding in an extrovert-dominated profession. This is completely untrue. There are plenty of professions in which introverts find their way to the top.

We think of acting as the most extroverted profession, yet there are plenty of actors who don't like to interact with people off of the movie set.

Introverts can find their own ways to succeed in extroverted markets. There are plenty of people with massive social media followings who have set up their accounts specifically so they do not have to interact with people in person.

My entire business is built around face-to-face communication, networking, talking with people, and forming relationships. I have learned to use my introversion as an advantage, and you can do the exact same thing in your profession if you just strategize.

5. We don't have social skills. This is a different way of saying the same thing: "Introverts are boring, shy, and don't like to talk to other people."

There is a grain of truth to this one. Sometimes, we feel anxiety because we do not know what to do in certain social situations. If we were sure of the right answer, we would say something.

We get into these situations of paralysis by analysis. You know you want to say something, but you are not sure how to say it to sound smart, cool, intelligent, or witty, so you don't say anything.

Extroverts are willing to say the wrong answer, but we are a little more conscientious and try to find the right answer. This is a small hurdle that we can overcome by developing our techniques and practicing.

6. We don't know how to have fun and enjoy ourselves. We know how to have fun. We just have introverted hobbies.

During my free time, I like to read books and hang out with my family. I have a really good time, but other people might perceive that as boring. We all experience the world in a different way.

It is okay to have some solitary hobbies, but it is also worth it to try to find some external or physical hobbies to expand your horizons. We have already developed a strategy for finding one of those great hobbies or activities to help you overcome this myth.

7. We need to become extroverts. This is probably the most common myth and the one that affects you the most. It is the idea that there is something wrong with you and that you need to change your personality to become more popular.

Introverts and extroverts recharge their batteries in different ways. I recharge mine by being by myself, while extroverts recharge theirs by being in social situations. I can only handle big groups for a couple of hours before I start to get bored, but I know plenty of people whose favorite way of networking is large group dinners.

You do not need to change who you are. You just need to find a balance between social and solo activities so that you can maintain your emotional energy.

Rather than change your personality, find your strengths and build on them. Trying to become an extrovert will not lead to greater success. It will just lead to discontinuity between how you feel on the inside how you act on the outside, and people will be able to pick up on that discontinuity.

8. Extroversion is normal, introversion is not. This myth is almost true. A larger percentage of the population is extroverted than introverted. But being the majority is not how we define normal.

It is the same as saying being right-handed is normal and being left-handed is abnormal. Back in Roman times, they believed that left-handed people were weird or even evil. The Latin word for left-handed is *sinister*.

We certainly do not believe that anymore. Ten percent of the population is too large of a percentage to be considered not normal.

Introverts might be in the minority of personality types,

but a society of only extroverts could never function. It would be like a gorilla colony, where everyone is shouting and no one is listening. Without introverts as part of the mechanism, all of the gears of society would seize up, and, eventually, the machine would explode.

9. We aren't happy. If you are quiet and your neutral face is even one percent frown, then people will assume that you are aloof, unpleasant, or unhappy.

People are always trying to observe and perceive your personality. They are trying to take your social temperature to see if you are happy, sad, or mad so they can react appropriately. When they misinterpret what is going on inside of you, they will apply the wrong tag.

There are certainly unhappy introverts in the world, but there are plenty of extroverted people who were also unhappy. Being introverted or extroverted has no correlation to your level of happiness.

We have now put together many mechanisms to help fight against your unhappiness. In addition to your social anxiety, you may also be dealing with issues of depression or procrastination. I have other books to help overcome those specific challenges, but you should try to deal with one challenge at a time. Conquer your social anxiety before you feel the need to jump into a different book and fight the next challenge.

10. We lack ambition. The highest level of confidence is not the loud, brash frat boy shouting. It is the person who is so assured of themselves that they do not need to talk about it.

I have known and worked with nearly a dozen members

of different Special Forces units, and not a single one of them felt the need to talk, brag, or be loud about it. The idea that these people lack ambition just because they don't brag about themselves is simply ridiculous.

There are a ton of movies and books about elite soldiers because they are so ambitious. With the combination of physical and mental fortitude that they endure, they do not need to shout that they are Navy SEALs, Marine Recon, or Green Berets. They just are, and that is the highest level of confidence.

You can be quiet and still be unbelievably ambitious. The truly smart people mask their ambition, and this is where you see the greatest success.

Myths Aren't Real

As inaccurate and unfair as these myths and stereotypes are, we can all agree that they are very prevalent in our culture. It would be nice to get rid of all these myths, but it is not going to happen anytime soon.

The purpose of discussing these myths is not to make you feel overwhelmed but to help you understand some of the thoughts that are out there. There are plenty of people who completely misunderstand us, and we need to accept that. Their perception of who we are does not matter in the long run.

Every once in a while, I get a review for one of my books from someone who clearly did not understand what I was talking about. They misinterpret both my motivation and the stories I shared. It does not feel great to get these reviews, but I understand that their review is not really about me. What they are doing is reviewing a misinterpretation.

When people misinterpret you, do not let that affect your sense of self-perception. Focus on the steps in front of you to achieve the progress you desire. Go piece by piece and just finish one step before you move on to the next.

Some people are going to be wrong. Some people are always going to misunderstand you, but you cannot invest your time or effort into that. Their misinterpretation cannot be what controls your entire destiny.

Instead of feeling overwhelmed by their misinterpretation, you need to be driven and motivated by your own successes. Do not allow yourself to be limited by the definitions or names other people call you. Other people are wrong all the time, and we must move beyond that.

Reflection Questions

Please answer the following questions in your Stop Shyness and Social Anxiety Journal:

1. Do any of these myths feel familiar?

2. Have any of these myths affected your sense of self-perception?

3. Have you ever been called any of these labels – boring, shy, introverted, not fun, unsociable, or socially awkward? How did it make you feel? Did you feel limited by that definition?

4. When you start to think of yourself as any of those negative labels, do you notice your behavior altering or changing? Do you notice that once someone calls you boring you start to feel a little bit more boring?

5. The next time someone calls you one of these labels, what are you going do to push back against it?

Activity

It is time to shatter the myth that you are boring. We do not tell stories or exciting adventures because we are afraid of bragging and we are not properly calibrated to the social situation. We think that if we tell a story, it could go wrong or backfire. We do not want to say things unless we are absolutely sure we will get the right response.

The only way to break through this is through experimentation rather than guesswork. We are going to build on our previous activity. You are going to go to the borders of your social experiences where you feel uncomfortable. You are going to do it in a no-risk situation – job interviews for jobs you do not want, meetups for groups you do not care about.

You are going to start telling stories and jokes that you think might be too far just to see what happens. You need to tell your best stories and your worst stories. All you are going to do is focus on people's responses.

I used to think my greatest story was the time I climbed a mountain in Japan, got lost, nearly died, and almost had to drink my own urine to survive. I thought that this was a story that shows how I can triumph over adversity. It is a story of success and thriving.

I discovered through experimentation that men find the story enthralling while women find the story disgusting. No woman will listen to me tell a story about how I almost drank my own urine to survive and then want to kiss me. It is an absolute attraction killer. Through experimentation, I found out that what I thought was my best story was actually my worst.

Once you get out there and start experimenting, you'll figure which of your stories are your best and which are your worst. Some of the stories you like to talk about will end up being the ones that people never want to hear about. Dreams, for example, are always boring, and no one wants to hear about them. If you like to talk about your dreams, stop it and start a dream journal instead.

Watch what other people are doing. Do people try to sneak away when you are telling a story? That means it is a bad story. Do you tell a joke that doesn't make people laugh? Sometimes there are jokes that don't fit in certain situations. The only way to calibrate yourself is through experience.

Wherever your border is, this is where you need to practice. If your border is talking to the same gender, then go talk to someone of the same gender. If your border is giving public speeches, then you need to put yourself into that environment.

You need to do this in a situation where there are no consequences. This way, when it is time to give a talk or lecture at work, you are ready to do it. Practicing in no-risk situations will allow you to overcome your social anxiety when you find yourself in a real situation.

9

BUILDING CONFIDENCE

We all know that confidence is important and attractive to others. People always say that being confident will get you what you want from life, but no one ever combines it with practical steps that you can implement to become more confident.

Advice without a structure for implementation is worthless. You can tell me to be confident, but if you do not tell me how to do it, it is not really useful advice.

In chapter three, we covered the advantages of being an introvert. Here is a review of those advantages.

1. We have introspective ability and self-awareness
2. We are deep thinkers and very creative
3. We have strong focus
4. We are independent
5. We think things through properly
6. We have more capacity for being visionaries
7. We prefer deep, meaningful conversation

8. We are better at influencing and persuasion than you think

9. We are excellent listeners and observers

10. We are excellent with written and detailed communications

TAKE A MOMENT TO ASSESS YOURSELF, focusing particularly on your strengths. When we spend all of our time focusing on our weaknesses, our confidence starts to diminish.

There are plenty of things I am terrible at, but you will notice that I rarely talk about them. I am aware of them, but they take up a very small part of my thoughts.

There is a ratio between thinking about your strengths and your weaknesses. The more you think about your weaknesses, the lower your confidence goes; the more you think more about your strengths, the faster your confidence will rise. We want to alter our thoughts and become more aware of the stronger parts of our personalities.

We are going to continue to build and strengthen your confidence, but first, it is important to make sure you know where you currently lie on the confidence spectrum.

In the next section, I have a little confidence test for you. Go through to get an idea of where you fall on the spectrum. Even if you're at the very top or the very bottom, it is worth finishing this chapter so you have a deep understanding of the process of building confidence.

Confidence Test

1. Usually, how willing are you to take a stand on something you feel is right that others won't approve of?

   a) Very often

b) Sometimes
c) Rarely

2. How willing are you to take risks that you feel could bring you real rewards?
   a) Very willing
   b) Somewhat willing
   c) Not willing

3. When you make a mistake, what is your most likely reaction?
   a) I will admit it and learn from it.
   b) I might admit to it. I'll likely learn from it.
   c) I'll do everything possible to cover it up, and/or I'll be in denial.

4. Do you ever catch yourself blatantly boasting about your accomplishments?
   a) No. I am proud of my accomplishments, but I never feel the need to boast.
   b) If I do, it's very rare.
   c) Yes, sometimes I feel I need to do so to feel better about myself.

5. What is your usual response when people compliment you?
   a) I graciously accept the compliment.
   b) I might be a little hesitant to accept it, but I usually do.

c) I usually protest and discount the compliment in some way.

For each a) answer, give yourself 3 points. For each b) answer, give yourself 2 points. For each c) answer, give yourself 1 point.

Scoring

11-15: You have a strong confidence level.

6-10: Your confidence level is generally good, but there is a significant amount of room for growth.

0-5: Your confidence level is currently low.

Now that you have a good, general idea of what your confidence level probably is, it's time to think about setting goals.

Setting Goals

If you have read any other self-help or personal development books, you have heard about goal-setting. I talk about this all the time because it is a critical component of this process. We often set goals that cannot be achieved because there is no way to measure them.

I had a discussion with a guy once who was on a similar path to me, struggling to find true love. We were talking about overcoming our social anxiety when talking to women. When I asked him what his goal was, he said he wanted to have a ton of great conversations with attractive women.

I said, "Let's imagine you hit that goal. This year, you have one million unbelievably in-depth and meaningful conversations with attractive women, but you do not get a single phone number, and none of them ever go on a date with you. Would you be happy with that result?" He said, "No, of course not."

Having conversations with attractive women wasn't his goal. Getting dates with attractive women was.

A goal is a measurable and achievable outcome that will make you happier. We want to have large-picture, long-term goals that are very clear and well defined. A goal is successful if it has a due date and we can measure it. "I want to talk to thirty people in thirty days." "I want to visit fifty states in twelve months."

Having a measurable number as well as a time frame for that goal will let us know if we achieved it or not. This will help us to break that goal into smaller, more attainable pieces.

If you want to talk to thirty people in thirty days, you already know that you need to talk to one person a day. If you want to go to fifty states in twelve months, you know you need to visit roughly one state each week.

If you can't break your goal into smaller and more manageable chunks, it will seem overwhelming and you will probably never reach that goal. Adding specific moments to your goal makes it easier to achieve.

As you achieve more goals, you are going to feel pretty good about yourself. When you feel proud of yourself for achieving so many goals, your confidence will start to rise.

If all we have are vague goals that we never achieve, we are obviously going to feel a bit like failures. The great thing about having a specific goal with smaller pieces is that each time we achieve one of those pieces we get that good feeling.

You should build specific goals around overcoming your social anxiety. "I want talk to ten strangers this month. I want to give a public speech once a month for the next year."

When you create goals that can be broken down and measured, you will achieve them faster. The more you achieve, the faster you will start to overcome your social anxiety and the better you will feel.

Monitor Your Thinking

As we move through this process, you can become extremely vulnerable. When you are modifying your personality or going through a period of transition, the things people say can really affect you.

Sometimes, the most powerful comments are those that come from within. When you are changing something about yourself, you might hear a little voice in your head saying, "You are no longer staying true to yourself." These little negative thoughts will block your progress.

Monitor your thoughts. When that negative voice creeps up, look in the mirror and tell that voice, "How can there possibly be a downside to wanting to be happier? I'm trying to have a better life and improve myself. Bad thought, get out of here. You are not welcome anymore."

The "Shy and Quiet" Label

You might already feel like you are trapped by these two labels. They are socially limiting and they are incredibly powerful. Once someone thinks of you in these terms, it is very difficult to break free.

There are certain words and phrases that take a great deal a verbal jujitsu to overcome, and I'm going to show you that technique now.

I'm Not Shy

When someone calls you shy, you have to take action immediately. Once the label sticks, you'll be stuck trying to dig your way out of the hole that you're already in. Instead of trying to escape with a shovel, you're going to use an advanced conversational technique called Frame Control and reverse with the other person said. Basically, you will make the phrase about them.

When someone calls you shy, say, "He thinks it is really funny to call me shy." This is taking that limiting word and using it against the person who said it.

Depending on your calibration, you could take it even further. "He likes to call me shy because he is a bit of a jerk." If you feel uncomfortable pushing it that far, a nice middle ground could be, "He likes to call me shy because he thinks that he is my high school bully. Isn't that adorable that he thinks we are still in high school?"

Look at the dynamics of this situation. He tried to trap you with a limiting label, and you reversed it, making the conversation about how he is a high school bully. This person has never heard your reverse before, so they haven't had the time to think of their own response. You've essentially taken their trap and set it on them.

The people that have heard this exchange will think that person is just a bully and dismiss it the next time he calls you shy or any other limiting word. Nothing he calls you will stick to you again.

I developed this technique because I was trapped by a label by someone for a long time. At first, I thought he was trying to limit me on purpose, but he really did not realize what he was doing. We had a talk about this; years and years later, I am still friends with him. Not everything is malicious.

You can reverse any social prison when you prepare yourself a little bit in advance.

Reflection Questions

Please answer the following questions in your Stop Shyness and Social Anxiety Journal:

1. Do you feel like we have enough techniques in this book for you to work on building up your confidence?

2. If you push back against stress, raise your self-esteem, and push back against your social anxiety, is that enough for you to raise your confidence? If not, what can you do to find more confidence-building techniques?

3. Which on the list of ten strong qualities of an introvert apply to you? Where are your strengths? Write them down and how they make you feel. Write out each strength, a specific example of when you demonstrated that strength, and how it made you feel in that situation.

4. How do you set goals? Have you been setting goals the right or the wrong way for most of your life? Have you been setting goals that you can achieve or setting goals that are impossible because they are not specific enough?

5. How do you feel about this verbal jujitsu technique of reversing it when someone calls you shy, introverted, or quiet? Do you understand why this technique works? Where on the social calibration spectrum do you find yourself? How far do you feel comfortable pushing?

Activity

The only way to learn how to fight is to get punched. You can read all the books in the world about fighting, but if you do not know what it feels like to get punched, you have no idea how to fight. The same goes for our social confidence. The only way to build it is to be in social environments.

As always, we're going to build on our previous activities. You are going to take your specific goals and implement everything from this chapter.

In the first activity of this book, we wrote down a list of the social situations where we were afraid and limited by our social anxiety. I want you to break down each of those situations into the smallest goals possible.

Start off by setting a specific goal. If your fear is public speaking, set down a specific long-term goal to help you with that fear. Remember, it has to be measurable and it has to have a due date. "I want to be able to give one speech without being afraid in six months."

Next, set a series of small goals in between now and then. Break it down into as many small pieces you can. The smaller the steps, the easier they are to achieve.

Once you have a clear long-term goal broken down into short-term goals, you will know what you need to achieve each day, week, and month. This will help grow your confidence because now you can focus on the process rather than the problem.

Let's say you have trouble meeting strangers in a business environment. You can set your goal as, "In six months, I want to be able to talk to an absolute business stranger, have a successful ten-minute conversation, and exchange business cards or phone numbers at the end."

We then break it into pieces. You have six months or 182 days to reach that goal, so you should have 182 small goals.

Start to go through the pieces of a conversation to help you figure out what your small goals should be. "The first thing I need to do is master hello. Every time I go out of the house, I need to say hello to ten strangers until it is no longer scary." That is goal number one.

Goal number two is the name exchange. "I want to get to a point where I can have a conversation with a stranger where we tell each other our names."

Go through the steps of a conversation to figure out what each of your small, daily goals should be. Put in place goal after goal until you have the structure of a successful conversation.

We then have our implementation. This is the hard part where you take your goals and actually follow through with them. If you have a goal of talking to ten people at a party, then you cannot leave that party until you have talked to ten people.

Whether this seems like an easy or a hard thing to do, I can tell you that is absolutely and totally achievable. If you break it down into smaller pieces, you will be successful in reaching your goals. This is a bit of a long-term project, but this is how you can shatter your social anxiety forever.

CONCLUSION

We have reached the end of this book, but we're just beginning your journey. Even after you put this book down, you can continue to implement many of the activities that I have shared with you. As you continue to modify your behavior, you'll notice changes in your life.

Social anxiety is one of the most common phobias in Western civilization, and you can overcome it as long as you stick with the lessons I've taught you.

If you have seen some of my other books, you know that some of them are three, four, or even five times longer than this one. This book is so short because I do not want you to spend all of your time reading. It is an isolationist activity that keeps you separate from other people.

The goal here is to give you enough tools and activities to get you out into the world and to implement the strategies I've given you. Your job now is to go back and work your way through the activities that you might have skipped over and to develop a strategy to get out into the world and overcome your social anxiety.

We all experience social anxiety in different ways, but

the process of overcoming and breaking through this challenge is the same. I know exactly what it is like to be afraid to talk to other people and grow your life and to worry that you are too shy. I was able to break through those labels, and now I'm far enough up the mountain that I can help you break through them as well.

You now know what to do if someone calls you shy or any other limiting label. You know the way to reverse that verbal assault and how to take back control of the conversation.

You no longer need to let other people's powerful and mean words define you. You are in charge of your destiny, and, as long as you implement this process, you will begin to experience more success.

I want you to know that you are never alone. I encourage you to join our Facebook group where other people are on the same journey. This group is a community where all the other people who follow me and who have been through similar experiences can communicate, commiserate, and share their experiences.

You have a group where you can share your ideas, get some feedback, and talk to other people who read this book. You can ask them questions, and they will know the answer because they have already experienced what you are experiencing now. This is the power of community.

We live in a modern world in which books are no longer written by someone who you will never be able to communicate with. This is the start of a conversation and now it is your turn to speak back to me. If you email me, message me on Facebook, or if you reach out in any other way, I will reply to you.

People are always surprised when I respond to them, but you must remember that this is a cooperative journey. I am happy to answer any questions you may have or help you through any activity that you may be stuck on.

If you are reading this on Kindle, you will have the opportunity to leave me a review shortly. All I ask is that you be honest. Even if you just click on five stars, that is enough to help me continue my business. I have poured my heart and soul out to you, and all I ask is that you give me back ten seconds of your time in return.

If you have skipped over the activities in the book, it can be hard for you to leave a review. You have the right to leave a negative review if you want, but I ask you to simply try the activities first. Please take the time to see if the material works for you, and, if it does not, then you have every right to leave me a bad review.

Every once in a while, I get a bad review from someone who read half the book and did not try any of the activities. They did not try.

If you are willing to try, I am willing to go with you. I am willing to continue this journey with you, communicate with you through the special group we have on Facebook or via email, and help to ensure your success. I am more invested in your success than anything else.

Work your way through the activities, give me ten seconds of your time, and leave an honest review so that other people can find this book and we can continue to grow our community and find more people to help. All of these things are part of our larger process and part of our goal to become better people and have better lives.

I am excited that you are now a member of my tribe and that you have read something that I have to say. I am deeply invested in your success. If you reach out to me, I will be there for you. If you reach out to other members of our community, they will be there for you. We are a very supportive bunch and we are excited to see people have better lives.

I cannot wait to see what the future holds for you. I cannot wait to see the results of your activities, hear about you shattering your social anxiety, and see you beginning to take control of your life.

When I was going through this journey, I wanted to never be afraid again. I wanted to be able to do the things my heart desired, and that is what I want for you. I want you to be able to give the speeches you want, to talk to the people you want to talk to, to go to job interviews without fear, and find the success that I know you deserve.

I am excited to see where the journey takes you, and I cannot wait to see what is coming next in your amazing life.

LET'S SOAR TOGETHER

The hardest part of personal growth is going it alone. When you are in isolation, the night can seem too dark, and success can seem so far away.

We often quit right before we could experience our biggest success. Join something bigger than yourself where you can get the support, feedback, and guidance you need to achieve your desired success.

Please join my FREE, private Facebook group, filled with supportive people on the same path.

https://servenomaster.com/community

This is a great place to chat with me daily, share your experiences with the exercises and find a supportive group of people who are all on the same journey as you.

MORE INFORMATION

Throughout this book, I mentioned other books, images, links, and additional content. All of that can be found at:

https://servenomaster.com/shy

You don't have to worry about trying to remember any other links or the names of anything mentioned in this book. Just enjoy the journey and focus on taking control of your destiny.

FOUND A TYPO?

While every effort goes into ensuring that this book is flawless, it is inevitable that a mistake or two will slip through the cracks.

If you find an error of any kind in this book, please let me know by visiting:

ServeNoMaster.com/typos

I appreciate you taking the time to notify me. This ensures that future readers never have to experience that awful typo. You are making the world a better place.

ABOUT THE AUTHOR

Born in Los Angeles, raised in Nashville, educated in London, Jonathan Green has spent years wandering the globe as his own boss – but it didn't come without a price. Like most people, he struggled through years of working in a vast, unfeeling bureaucracy.

After the backstabbing and gossip of the university system threw him out of his job, he was devastated – stranded far away from home without a paycheck coming in. Despite having to hang on to survival with his fingernails, he didn't just survive; he thrived.

Today, he says that getting fired with no safety net was the best thing that ever happened to him. Despite the stress, it gave him an opportunity to rebuild and redesign his life.

One year after being on the edge of financial ruin, Jonathan had replaced his job, working as a six-figure SEO consultant. With his Rolodex overflowing with local businesses and their demands getting higher and higher, he knew that he had to take his hands off the wheel.

That's one of the big takeaways from his experience. Lifestyle design can't just be about a job replacing income, because often, you're replicating the stress and misery that comes with that lifestyle too!

Thanks to smart planning and personal discipline, he started from scratch again, with a focus on repeatable, passive income that created lifestyle freedom. He was more successful than he could have possibly expected. He traveled the world, helped friends and family, and moved to an island in the South Pacific.

Now, he's devoted himself to breaking down every hurdle entrepreneurs face at every stage of their progress, from developing mental strength and resilience in the depths of depression and anxiety, to developing financial and business literacy, to building a concrete plan to escape the 9-to-5, all the way down to the nitty-gritty details of teaching what you need to build a business of your own.

In a digital world packed with "experts," there are few people with the experience to tell you how things really work, why they work and what actually works in the online business world.

Jonathan doesn't just have the experience; he has it in a variety of spaces. A bestselling author, a "ghostwriter to the gurus" who commands sky-high rates due to his ability to deliver captivating work in a hurry, and a video producer who helps small businesses share their skills with their communities.

He's also the founder of the Serve No Master podcast, a weekly show focused on financial independence, networking with the world's most influential people, writing epic stuff online and traveling the world for cheap.

Altogether, it makes him one of the most captivating and accomplished people in the lifestyle design world, sharing the best of what he knows with total transparency, as part of a mission to free regular people from the 9-to-5 and live on their own terms.

Learn from his successes and failures and Serve No Master.

Find out more about Jonathan at:
ServeNoMaster.com

BOOKS BY JONATHAN GREEN

Non-Fiction

Serve No Master Series

Serve No Master

Serve No Master (French)

Breaking Orbit

20K a Day

Control Your Fate

BREAKTHROUGH (coming soon)

Habit of Success Series

PROCRASTINATION

Influence and Persuasion

Overcome Depression

Stop Worrying and Anxiety

Love Yourself

Conquer Stress

Law of Attraction

Mindfulness and Meditation Ultimate Guide

Meditation Techniques for Beginners

I'm Not Shy

Coloring Depression Away with Adult Coloring Books

Don't be Quiet

Social Skills

Many Anyone Like You

Develop Good Habits with S.J. Scott

How to Quit Your Smoking Habit

The Weight Loss Habit

Seven Secrets

Seven Networking Secrets for Jobseekers

Biographies

The Fate of my Father

Complex Adult Coloring Books

The Dinosaur Adult Coloring Book

The Dog Adult Coloring Book

The Celtic Adult Coloring Book

The Outer Space Adult Coloring Book

Irreverent Coloring Books

Dragons Are Bastards

Fiction

Gunpowder and Magic

The Outlier (As Drake Blackstone)

ONE LAST THING

Reviews are the lifeblood of any book on Amazon, especially for the independent author. If you would click five stars on your Kindle device or visit this special link at your convenience, that will ensure that I can continue to produce more books. A quick rating or review helps me to support my family, and I deeply appreciate it.

Without stars and reviews, you would never have found this book. Please take just thirty seconds of your time to support an independent author by leaving a rating.

Thank you so much!

To leave a review go to ->

https://servenomaster.com/shyreview

Sincerely,
Jonathan Green
ServeNoMaster.com